FROM EMPTY CHAIRS
TO BUSY OPD

The Practical Marketing Guide for Doctors

FROM EMPTY CHAIRS TO BUSY OPD

The Practical Marketing Guide for Doctors

NITYANAND RUNGTA

Available on amazonkindle

Worldwide Published by

Pendown Press

PREMIUM BUSINESS PUBLISHER

PENDOWN PRESS LLP
An ISO 9001 & ISO 14001 Certified Co.,
Regd. Office: 3767A, Kanhaiya Nagar,
Tri Nagar, Delhi-110035
Ph.: 8130886000, 9650072927
E-mail: info@pendownpress.com
Branch Office: 1A/2A, 20, Hari Sadan, Ansari Road,
Daryaganj, New Delhi-110002
Ph.: 011-45794768
Website: PendownPress.com

Edition: 2025
Price: ₹ 299
ISBN: 978-93-7217-260-7

Layout and Cover Designed by Pendown Graphics Team
Printed and Bound in India by Thomson Press India Ltd.

CONTENTS

ACKNOWLEDGEMENTS i

PREFACE: Why This Book Exists iii
Why You Can Trust It

FOREWORD 1 xi

FOREWORD 2 xiii

HOW TO USE THIS BOOK xv

CHAPTER 1

The First Big Mistake That's Killing Your OPD 1

CHAPTER 2

The Funnel That Built a 92% Return Rate 11

CHAPTER 3

From Second Visit to Superfan: 27
The Silent Engine of OPD Growth

CHAPTER 4

Redesigning Your Clinic Experience 37
Without Spending a Fortune

CHAPTER 5

The Online OPD: 47
Where Trust Is Built Before Entry

CHAPTER 6

Turning Your Social Media into a Silent OPD Builder 55

CHAPTER 7

What Your Patients Really Want: 61
But Never Say Out Loud

ACKNOWLEDGEMENTS

This book was never just about marketing. It was about reclaiming the dignity of good doctors who've been left behind in a noisy world. And I couldn't have written it without a few key people who shaped every page sometimes with insights, sometimes with brutal honesty.

To my father, Shri Rash Behari Rungta, for building a legacy where ethics were never a trade-off. Watching him handle every patient with calm clarity and unwavering compassion taught me that integrity isn't negotiable.

To our frontline staff at Rungta Hospital receptionists, call center executives, housekeeping, nursing, and pharmacy. Every time I sat next to you, observed your work, and listened to patient stories, I saw the real gaps. And the real possibilities.

To the 500+ doctors, consultants and visiting surgeons who spoke openly with me often sharing uncomfortable truths, you shaped this book more than you realize. Every frustration you shared became a framework. Every doubt you raised became a chapter.

To the disease that changed everything pancreatitis. I never thought I'd be thankful for an illness, but it gave me the one thing no MBA, no strategy session, no marketing workshop could give me: the perspective of a patient. The helplessness. The hope. The waiting. The fear. It made me understand what truly matters to patients and what doctors often miss. Without that experience, this book would have been just theory

To my mentors, India's top marketing coaches and trainers who taught me to think deeper than just campaigns. You helped me see that healthcare marketing isn't about visibility, it's about trust.

And finally, to the doctors who feel tired, unseen, or underappreciated you were in my mind with every sentence I wrote. This book is my way of telling you: the world needs to see you. And now, they will.

PREFACE

WHY THIS BOOK EXISTS AND WHY YOU CAN TRUST IT

Hi, I'm Nityanand Rungta, and I am the Strategic Head of Rungta Hospital, Jaipur.

And before you wonder who this 19-year-old is telling me how to grow my OPD, let me be upfront.

Yes, I'm young. But I've spent over 5,000 hours in one-on-one training with India's best marketing and operations coaches across India. I didn't just do a few online courses. I learned directly from the source, mentors who consult the top businesses in India by sitting across from them, asking them what really works, and testing it myself.

And then I combined that knowledge with something few marketers ever have: real, raw insights from healthcare.

Over the past year, I've spent 1200+ hours personally interviewing patients and sat down with more than 500 of the best doctors across India, from tier-1 cities to rural belts. I wanted to crack one key problem:

Why were so many great doctors struggling to grow their OPD, even though they're delivering excellent care?

It wasn't a lack of skill. It wasn't ethics. It wasn't attitude.

The problem was this: Young doctors are buried in service. In rounds, emergencies, academics, family pressure, and patient load, they're never taught how to brand themselves or run a practice like a system. And in that gap, agencies and self-declared marketers walk in, flash a few reports, drop jargon, and walk away with their money.

The doctor waits, hopes, and six months later sees zero impact.

But something even deeper pushed me to do this. Under my father's guidance, someone who rebuilt a struggling hospital over 14 years into a thriving institution. I got the rare chance to meet what I call the **"James Bonds" of the medical industry**. Doctors who have cracked the code. People who have enhanced their excellent medical skills with brilliant systems. I sat with them. I listened. I learned.

In my conversations with senior doctors, I realized something important. **The old ABC formula** that many in the industry still talk about: A for Availability, B for Behavior, and C for Competence, **no longer works on its own.** Times have changed, and so have patient expectations.

Today, this formula needs an upgrade. I call it AB3C. The A and B remain the same: Availability and Behavior.

But instead of jumping straight to Competence, we now need to add two more Cs before it: Communication and Credibility. Only then does Competence take its rightful place.

So the new order is: Availability, Behavior, Communication, Credibility, and finally Competence. Notice something important here: competence, the one thing most doctors focus on, actually comes third. Yet most doctors I meet are focused on polishing their skills and knowledge, while overlooking how they are perceived by patients. And perception, in today's world, is often what determines whether a patient chooses to return or not.

The AB3C Success Framework for Doctors

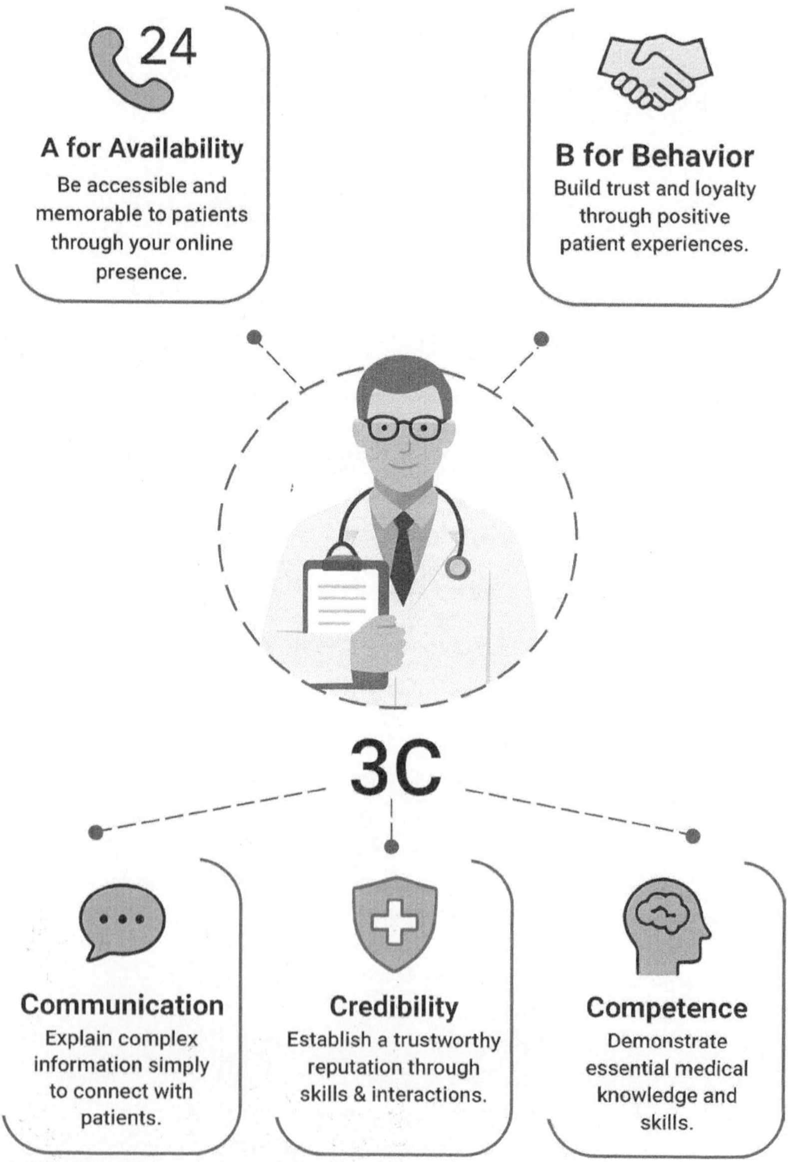

They forget that in today's world, people choose who they remember. Not just who is qualified.

One of the turning points for me was a conversation I had during an interview with a senior physician, Dr Goyal, in a Tier 2 city. He had decades of experience, a loyal set of patients, and yet his OPD had stopped growing.

He told me, people seem to come to a doctor when they are suffering from a cold, cough, fever, etc., or when things get out of hand and they can no longer manage without a doctor. I want to encourage them to come for regular follow-ups for diseases like diabetes, hypertension, etc.; however, they never seem to return. And I have absolutely no idea why, because they find the treatment, ambience, and staff good.

I listened to him, and then I shared a few small but specific tips and a framework, which are also in this book.

Two weeks later, he messaged me. "I don't know what kind of magic you shared, but my old patients started coming back, and new walk-ins have also increased."

It wasn't magic. It was clarity. That's what this book gives you.

That's when it clicked for me. With my father by my side, and with a deep gratitude for doctors who carry the weight of saving lives, **I decided to write this book.**

The intent behind this book is to bring together everything I've learned from the mentors, the doctors, the patients, and our own hospital's transformation, So that dedicated, excellence-oriented doctors don't have to struggle with a lack of systems anymore.

Why I Understand the Patient Side Better Than Most

This journey wasn't just academic for me. I was born in 2006, and by the age of five, I was diagnosed with pancreatitis, a rare, painful condition that led to more than 40 hospital admissions over 11 years. I was a long-term patient, trying everything: Ayurveda, Allopathy, Unani, you name it.

Coming from a hospital-owning family didn't spare me. I've seen how patients feel when they're waiting, misunderstood, or when attendants feel helpless. I've seen how a careless receptionist can undo the trust a doctor builds in 10 minutes. And I've seen how no one really asks patients what they feel, what scares them, or what would make things better.

I carried those scars. Until COVID changed everything.

I overheard my grandfather tell my father, who was worried about stepping into the hospital during peak COVID:

"Tume kuch ho gaya toh bhi koi baat nahi. Tum kisi ke kaam aaye."

(Even if something happens to you, it's okay, at least you were of help to someone.)

That line didn't just hit me. It woke me up.

From that moment, I made a decision. To stop being the patient. And start helping people who help people.

I immersed myself in marketing, operations, branding, human psychology, and everything I learned, I applied to Rungta Hospital, a 34-year-old institution that pioneered ICU, ICU on Wheels, and NICU services in private healthcare in Rajasthan. Slowly, I started seeing how the right systems could create transformation.

What You'll Get from This Book

This book is not just theory.

It's built on the shoulders of:

- Real-world doctor interviews and their valuable insights
- Patient psychology research
- My personal mentorship from India's top marketing experts
- Hours of trial-and-error in an actual hospital setting

Here's what you'll get:

- Why most digital marketing fails for doctors, and how to fix it
- How to turn your clinic into a patient magnet without spending a fortune
- Techniques to improve follow-ups, convert inquiries, and build recall
- A step-by-step method to turn patients into fans who refer others
- The 4W Framework I developed to uncover what patients really want, but never say out loud
- The time-traps that drain your energy, and how to reclaim your productivity

By the end, you'll have a complete system to 3X your OPD ethically, efficiently, and with empathy.

A Personal Note to You

I didn't write this book to prove something.

I wrote it because I've seen how hard you work, how deeply you care about the well-being of your patients, how you upgrade yourself with CME, and yet how little guidance and support exist for doctors in building system-driven, sustainable OPDs.

I've sat in the waiting rooms. I've seen patients walk away confused. I've seen clinics with great intent but broken systems. And I've seen that most of these problems are fixable once you understand the rules of visibility, experience, and trust.

This book is my way of saying:

You deserve to grow. And you don't have to figure it all out alone.

So whether you're just starting out or already established, this book will give you clarity, structure, and action.

It will help you build a practice that reflects the excellence you already bring to your patients.

Let's begin.

Nityanand Rungta

FOREWORD 1

When Nityanand first shared a draft of this book, I expected the usual marketing advice repackaged for doctors. But what I found instead was a strategic blueprint rooted in empathy, psychology, and deep respect for the medical profession.

"**From Empty Chairs to Busy OPD**" is not just a book but a wake-up call.

It highlights the silent reasons as to why great doctors often go unnoticed and their talent remains unappreciated.

It shows, with great clarity and conviction, how to fix that ethically, sustainably, and with the trust of the patients intact.

This book is all the more valuable because it doesn't just talk about numbers or promotions but about their (patients') emotions, recall, and behavior. It's rare to find someone who can think like a strategist and empathize like a patient.

If you're a doctor who believes good work should speak for itself, this book will help make sure it actually does.

Looking into the paucity of time, this book very deftly makes an impactful contribution not only for medical professionals but for anyone who wants to delve deeper in this area. I wish him all the best and look forward to many more contributions like this.

Prof. (Rtd) Harsh Dwivedi,

Ex Dean and Director R.A. Podar Institute of Management, University of Rajasthan, Jaipur

FOREWORD 2

Having seen an atmosphere of entrepreneurship right from birth with my grandfather being associated with it and then watching other evolving industries, both in mining, manufacturing, contracting, etc, I very closely observed that Healthcare is among the few service industries, where trust and transformation must go hand in hand.

This book is an expression of that and delivers.

Nityanand Rungta, a third-generation healthcare entrepreneur, combines inherited wisdom with hard-earned marketing insight, which makes his work exceptional and, in a true sense, worth emulating in Practice. It's not merely theory but a step-by-step guide underlining real patient psychology, ethical practices, and operational clarity.

This book is not just about filling chairs. It's about creating systems that inspire and recall referrals, and demonstrate reputation without resorting to other gimmicks.

For every doctor who wants to grow their OPD while staying true to their values, this book is a must-read. It offers clarity in a space that is surrounded by confusion.

I congratulate Nityanand on this contribution. It's an eye-opening and honest submission.

This will pave the way for how healthcare is practiced in the years to come.

Rahul Mahnot

former CEO Birla White (Ultratech Cement Ltd) and management consultant

HOW TO USE THIS BOOK

This book is not meant to be read and kept on a shelf.

It's meant to sit on your desk, beside your stethoscope.

Each chapter in this book is designed like a tool: Something you can pick up, apply, and see results. Some tools will show impact in 24 hours. Others, over 24 weeks. But every single one is tried, tested, and made for real-world doctors—not textbook marketers.

Here's how to get the most from it:

1. **Start where you feel the pain.**

   You don't have to read this cover to cover. If patient retention is your problem, start there. If your reception experience feels broken, jump to that chapter.

2. **Implement one thing at a time.**

   Marketing is not a "launch one campaign and wait" game. It's a layered strategy. Pick one thing, apply it fully. Then return for the next.

3. **Write in this book.**

   Take notes. Scribble ideas. Mark pages. This is your playbook.

4. **Discuss with your team.**

   Many of these strategies only work when your staff is aligned. Use chapters like "Clinic Experience Redesign" and "BIC Framework" to have open discussions with your staff, front desk, or even your digital agency.

If you follow just 30% of what's inside this book consistently, your OPD will not stay empty for long.

1

CHAPTER

THE FIRST BIG MISTAKE THAT'S KILLING YOUR OPD

So let's start with the first and the most important thing.

What's that one mistake that silently eats up your OPD growth?

It's this:

> **You are brilliant at your work, you care deeply for your patients, but you don't have a follow-up strategy.**

According to studies, nearly 80 percent of patients never return to the same doctor. Not because your treatment wasn't good, but because they forgot.

There's no system that reminds them to come back.

Think about it. Every person is bombarded with more than 4,000 ads every single day. Out of those, at least 80 are related to healthcare. There are countless options flashing in front of them.

- How can they remember you?
- How can they come back to you?
- Unless you stay in their consideration set?

That's why I created a simple but powerful concept called "BIC" – Be In Consideration.

This is not a digital campaign. It's not just a reminder text. It's a full framework designed to make sure that when your patient needs help again, your name is the first one that comes to mind.

Let me tell you a story about how this was wrongly used.

At Rungta Hospital, we have a simple rule: no doctor should ever feel unsupported. That's why I personally meet doctors regularly, not to promote, but just to listen. What are they struggling with? Where are patients dropping off?

In one of these conversations, I shared the BIC idea with a doctor. He liked it but misunderstood the core. He started sending festival greetings to patients, Diwali wishes, Holi messages, and so on. While it was better than doing nothing, he didn't see any real growth in OPD. While it's nice, it doesn't solve the real issue. It doesn't build recall. It doesn't help the patient. It becomes spam.

Why? Because the content wasn't useful. It wasn't relevant. It didn't build value or trust.

This strategy is not about complicated software or paid promotions. It's about staying in your patient's mind without being pushy.

So, let me decode this for you. The BIC strategy starts with identifying where your audience actually is. Are they on Facebook? WhatsApp? SMS? Radio? Or is it something else?

Now take a moment and think.

Where is your audience really present?

Write down your 10 lines below. Take your time.

____

____

____

____

____

____

____

____

____

____

Now, as you identify the platform, the second step is even more important.

What kind of content would actually be helpful for them? What kind of message would make them say, "This doctor really knows what he's doing"?

You already have the Knowledge and Skills, but what is the content that gets them to see that-

"This doctor is really knowledgeable and has the skills to relieve sickness."

The mistake we generally make is thinking any content is good content. But patients don't care about a generic post.

They care about how you can help them. That's it.

So here's how you should think about your content.

Three types of content truly work.

- **The first type is educational content.** Give solutions to problems. For example, if you are a general physician, send a short video or message like "3 simple ways to avoid heatstroke this summer" or "5 daily habits that help keep your blood pressure in control." This positions you as someone who truly cares and adds value.
- **The second type is awareness-based content.** Share updates about what is new in your field. Say, if you are a diabetologist, and a new nasal insulin is being tested globally, share that news. Even if you don't offer it yet, it shows you're updated. Patients start thinking, "My doctor is smart. He knows what's coming next." That's the image you want to build.
- **The third is trend-based content.** Let's say it's winter and a new viral infection is spreading. Make a quick video explaining the symptoms and protection tips. Patients will thank you. Because now, they feel you're not just treating them, you're protecting them.

Or even if you aren't able to figure out the right way, don't worry, ask your patients directly what type of medical-related content they would like to see or read

Let me share a quick story. During my own learning journey, I joined a big marketing course online. The coach never knew me personally, but I started trusting him and following his advice. Later in a live session, someone asked him, "Why do we all trust you so much even though we've never met?" He replied, "People love the person who is useful to them." **That's the secret. Be useful, and you'll be loved.**

So now ask yourself what kind of content would make your patients say "Wow"?

Write down your 10 lines here. Think clearly.

____

____

____

____

____

____

____

____

____

____

Now, let me share one of the most practical hacks I discovered. Even if your content is good, how will you deliver it if you don't have your patient's number saved, or if they haven't saved yours?

So the moment a patient visits you, ensure you save their number and they save yours too.

But here's the key. You are busy serving people, so it would be helpful if your phone could help you remember certain things:

When you save their number, add a small note about them, like-

"Mr. Mehta came for high BP; his son is studying in Delhi." The next time they call, you already know who they are and can speak with personal warmth. That memory creates magic.

Now, what if they haven't saved your number? Don't worry. At the end of the consultation, say:

"If you ever need me urgently, please text me at this number. Just give me a missed call once so I can save your number too. I don't usually see unknown messages, but I don't want to miss your message if you ever need help."

That's it. A simple script that builds trust and gets the job done.

Once the number is saved, add them to your broadcast list or WhatsApp group based on their condition, for example, a BP group, a sugar group, or a women's wellness group. Keep it useful, light, and never spammy.

Remember, don't assign this to your staff. You have to do it personally. This is about building a relationship, not ticking off a task. **And relationships are what grow your OPD.**

How a Senior Physician in Jaipur Brought His Patients Back by BIC

A senior physician in Jaipur was puzzled. His patients seemed satisfied, his treatment worked, and yet very few returned for follow-ups. At first, he assumed it was because they had fully recovered. But when I asked him to casually check with a few old patients, the reality shocked him.

One patient admitted,

"Doctor saab, main bhool gaya tha kab aana hai. Phir mere neighbor ne ek aur clinic suggest kar diya, toh wahan chala gaya."

(Doctor, I forgot when to come back. Then my neighbor suggested another clinic, so I went there.)

Another said,

"Doctor, maine aapka number save hi nahi kiya tha. Jab phir problem hui, toh Google kiya aur jo clinic paas mein dikha, wahan chala gaya."

(Doctor, I hadn't saved your number. When the issue came back, I just Googled and went to whichever clinic was nearby.)

Hearing this, the doctor was stunned.

- **Patients weren't leaving because of dissatisfaction.**
- **They were not coming back because of forgetfulness and convenience.**

That's when I introduced him to the **BIC framework—Be In Consideration**. He understood that being good at treatment wasn't enough. He had to make sure he was present in the patient's mind when the need arose again.

He decided to try it.

He began doing three things:

Saved every patient's number with a short note.

Ensured patients saved his number too, by saying, ***"Agar kabhi emergency ho toh direct yahan message karna. Lekin ek missed call de dena, taki main aapka number save kar loon."*** (If there's ever an emergency, message me here. Just give me a missed call once so I can save your number too.)

Instead of only sending generic "Happy Diwali" or "Good Morning" messages, he sent short, practical tips like: ***"Subah uthkar yeh ek aadat apnao, BP control rahega"*** (Adopt this one habit every morning to control BP) or ***"Sugar badhne ke yeh 3 signs kabhi ignore mat karo"*** (Never ignore these 3 signs of rising sugar).

Within weeks, patients started coming back.

Many even told him openly:

- *"Doctor saab, aapka message aaya toh yaad aaya ki check-up karana hai."* (Doctor, when I got your message, I remembered I had to come for a check-up.)
- "Good, you sent that BP tip, *warna main to bhool hi gaya tha aapke paas aane ka."* (Good that you sent that BP tip, otherwise I had completely forgotten to visit you.)
- *"Doctor, aapka message padha toh yaad aaya ki meri wife ko bhi leke aana hai, usko bhi same problem hai."* (Doctor, when I read your message, I remembered I should bring my wife too, she has the same issue.)

In just six months, his OPD retention improved by 28%. Not only did his old patients return, but many also brought their family members along.

What he realized was simple: patients don't drift away because they are dissatisfied with the treatment; they drift away because the doctor is not in their minds when they are next needed.

However, by being present in their daily lives with useful reminders, he became the first name they thought of when they needed care.

2

CHAPTER

THE FUNNEL THAT BUILT A 92% RETURN RATE

If you applied the BIC strategy from Chapter 1, you've already started planting seeds in your patient's mind. But awareness alone is not enough.

Just because someone sees your name doesn't mean they will walk into your clinic. You're not just battling other clinics, you're battling doubt, noise, distractions, and forgetfulness.

In fact, what I realized after observing thousands of patient journeys at Rungta Hospital is this: **patients don't transform into loyalists overnight.** They pass through an emotional and psychological journey, a funnel often without even realizing it. And if even one step is broken, they quietly exit without ever telling you why.

I didn't learn this from textbooks or marketing theory. I learned it the hard way by sitting with patients, understanding their unspoken thoughts, listening to their confusion, and watching what made them return or never come back.

Over time, a clear 5-stage pattern emerged as **a predictable path th**at every patient walks through, consciously or unconsciously, before becoming a loyal follower.

I call this path to loyalty the ACCRF Funnel. If you understand how to guide your patients through each of these stages with intention and empathy, your OPD won't just grow; it will become unstoppable.

You must understand one simple truth:

Patients don't jump from "stranger" to "loyalist" in one step.

There is a psychological journey every patient goes through before they become your fan. You're not competing with other doctors.

- You're competing with **forgetfulness**, **information overload**, and **"scroll culture."**
- The human brain deletes **non-urgent, non-emotional information**. So, unless you create **emotional urgency**, your name vanishes.

This journey has **5 stages** that I discovered while working deep in Rungta Hospital. I cracked the code by interviewing patients and changing the journey, and now at Rungta hospital, 92% of patients who come become fans. It was a difficult journey. Many things have changed just so that we will be useful to our patients and doctors.

This strategy is the **ACCRF Funnel**. It means awareness, consideration, consultation, retention, and then becoming a fan.

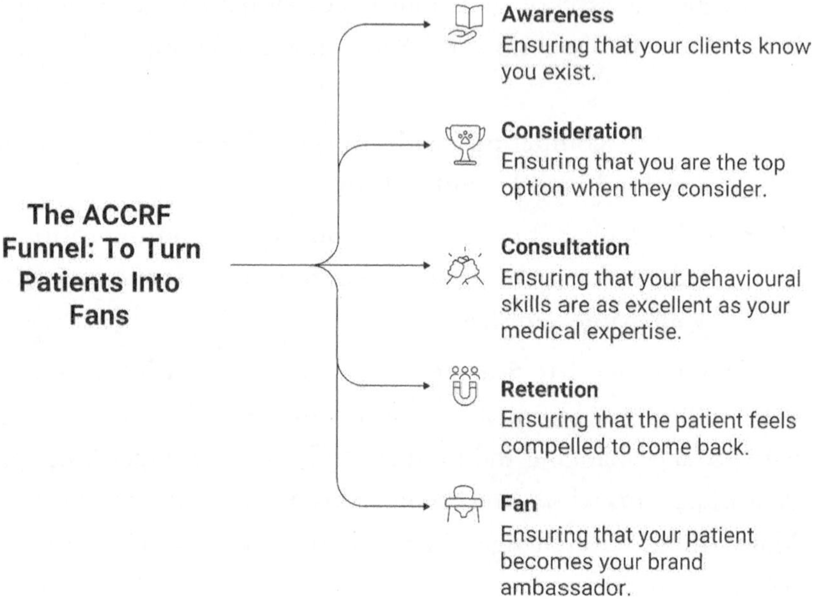

If you fix each stage, your OPD will grow naturally and powerfully, and your patient will surely become a die-hard fan. So let me decode how to do so.

Stage 1- Awareness

So in the first stage, which is awareness, which means **"Who are you?"** As I told you, a person in a day goes through 4000 ads, so you are visible to them? Also, if we consider that you are, what are you doing so that you are highlighted in the minds of the patients among the 4000+ ads they are seeing? When I interviewed recognized and reputed doctors in India, I understood a pattern. Most doctors think a clinic board is enough. Or they believe "*Agar ilaj acha hoga toh patients khud aayenge.*" (When the treatment is good, patients will come back for sure) But the real truth is the patients can't trust what they can't see.

Also, there is another perception, **"I'll hire a digital agency,"** but the dark reality is that **most agencies know social media. They don't know patient psychology.**

You must lead the message, even if they run the campaign.

So you would have to be visible on all platforms where your patient is available and seeing your competitors.

Let's go inside the mind of a patient for a moment.

Take a 35-year-old woman dealing with fatigue and mood swings. **She's not thinking, "I need an endocrinologist now."** She's thinking, **"Why am I always tired?"** or "Is something wrong with my hormones?" She's scrolling Instagram at night, hoping something will resonate. If she sees a reel that says, *"This one deficiency can mimic depression, are you missing it?"* she stops.

That's what I call a CCB — a Crowd Control Bomb.

A line that hooks attention and makes the patient want to know more. This is what awareness needs, not just clinic boards and photos, but **emotionally relevant messaging** that interrupts daily life.

You need to be on platforms your patients are already using: **Google, Instagram, WhatsApp, and local society groups.** But you need to do this interestingly, not with generic messages like "We care for you." Instead, you need curiosity-triggering content that reflects their pain, doubt, or daily struggle.

A board that says *"Free BP Check-up"* is okay. But one that says *"BP normal hai, par heart attack ka risk high hai?"* that makes people pause.

Your goal at this stage is simple: become **recognizable and relatable**. When someone says your name, the patient should say,

"Yes, I've seen their video," or "I've heard about that clinic near the main road." That's when awareness is working. You can build this using four simple tools:

- **First, optimize your Google My Business profile**, add photos, reviews, videos, working hours, and a short MCB in your description.
- **Second, post short, sharp Instagram reels or WhatsApp videos** with a clear hook, like *"Don't ignore this subtle sign of thyroid."*
- **Third, put boards or posters near high-footfall areas** like pharmacies, salons, gyms, and schools, not just near hospitals.
- **And finally, conduct micro-camps and health talks** with specific titles like *"Kya aapki thakan vitamin D ki wajah se hai?" (Is Vitamin D the reason behind your fatigue?)* instead of just "Free check-up.

I am sharing with you all the strategies we use at Rungta Hospital because h**ere we do our best to make every doctor in Rungta Hospital a star doctor with the impact that they and their patients deserve**.

For example, we are privileged to have an excellent neurosurgeon whose skills we showcased with YouTube videos using the CCB technique, offering value-added content to his target audience. He started getting 10-30k views on each video, and he became popular on social media. We also encouraged him to start a podcast, and that worked wonders. His visibility made people aware of his brilliance, and we started receiving 15-20 calls every day for him.

Remember, patients don't make appointments with people they don't know.

Your content, online or offline, must match their inner dialogue. When they're asking, *"Is this normal?"* Your reel or hoarding should say, *"It might not be."*

To check whether your awareness quotient is strong, ask yourself:

- Do you have more than 20 Google reviews?
- Do you post CCB-based content at least twice a week?
- Do local chemists and society guards know your name?

If not, then no matter how good your treatment is, you're **leaking attention** at the very first stage.

To make sure you're always visible, here's a simple weekly awareness ritual:

- On Mondays, post one CCB-based reel.
- On Wednesdays, share a patient review or story via WhatsApp.
- On Fridays, request Google reviews from two happy patients.
- And on Sundays, send an educational health message to local groups.

Repeat this for 6 weeks, and watch as awareness transforms into action.

Because **if the patient doesn't see you, they'll never choose you.** This stage may seem small — but it's the gatekeeper to your entire ACCRF funnel.

Once a patient becomes aware of your existence from a board, reel, or a WhatsApp message, they don't immediately book an appointment.

Stage 2- Consideration

They enter the other step, which is the **consideration stage**, where they silently ask, ***"Can I really trust this doctor with my body? My child? My future?"***

This stage is not logical; it's emotional. The patient is not looking for the "most qualified doctor." **They're looking for someone who feels safe**, **genuine**, and **relatable**. In fact, most patients decide within seconds of seeing your online or offline presence whether they feel "drawn" to you, and they'll start **collecting signs** to justify their decision.

So what are they doing at this stage? They're **stalking you**, **gently and quietly**.

- They'll Google your name.
- They'll check if you're on Google Maps and how many stars you have.
- They'll look for real patient reviews, not polished testimonials, but stories that sound like their own.
- They'll scroll through your Instagram or Facebook to see what kind of doctor you are: warm or cold, human or transactional, silent or someone who explains things.
- They might even ask their cousin in the neighborhood, *"Suna hai Dr. Arora ke baare mein? Kaise hain?"*

Here's where most doctors may lose the advantage: they have nothing prepared for this stage. They either post "Happy

Diwali" images that look like every other clinic, or they write dry bios: *"MBBS, MD, DM, 25 years experience."* That builds *credibility*, not *connection*. **And connection is what converts.**

What patients are actually looking for are signals of trust. They want to see someone like themselves in your content, maybe a short video of a mother saying, *"I was scared when my daughter had seizures, but this doctor made me feel calm."* Or a post showing, *"This is what 30 days of sugar control can do, shared with permission from Mr. Pankaj, 52."* They want to know that someone before them felt lost, got help, and came out stronger — all with you by their side.

The best tools at this stage are testimonials, transformation stories, short videos, and educational reels that show your expertise without arrogance.

- For example, instead of saying, "We specialize in liver care," post a 30-second clip saying: "Most people ignore right-side stomach pain, but it could be early liver damage. Here's how to spot it early." You've just given value before they walked in, and that builds deep trust.
- Another powerful strategy is to show your human side even in subtle ways. A picture of you tying a child's shoelace post-consultation, a quick reel explaining why you give every patient at least 60 seconds to speak without interruption, or a handwritten message saying, "If you're scared, it's okay, most patients are. You're not alone." These moments tell the patient: "This doctor is not just smart - they're safe."

- Also, don't underestimate the power of **visual cues**. Your clinic photos, staff uniforms, and even your logo all signal safety or risk. A clean, smiling front desk photo builds more confidence than ten degrees on a wall.
- And then come the **reviews**. If your Google page has fewer than 10 reviews, or worse, no recent ones, the patient's brain says: *"This clinic is either too new, too bad, or too empty."* Aim for 50+ authentic reviews. After every good consultation, train your staff to gently ask:
- "If you're feeling better and have a minute, would you mind leaving a short review? It helps others trust us, too." Make it easy, give them a direct, clickable link. And post one or two every week on your Instagram/Facebook stories.

Remember, the goal at this stage is not to "sell." It's to earn permission.

To make the patient feel like, *"This doctor gets me. They've helped people like me. I'm in good hands."* And once that emotional trust is established, booking an appointment becomes a natural next step.

If Stage 1 is about being seen, then Stage 2 is about being felt. Because patients don't walk into your clinic just because they saw an ad, they walk in because something about you made them **believe**.

Stage 3- Consultation

By the time a patient walks into your clinic or hospital, they've already gone through an emotional maze: anxiety, online research, a few recommendations, maybe even self-diagnosis. But even now, they haven't fully decided whether they'll come back to you.

That decision is made in the next 10 minutes, not based on your medical degree, but on how you make them feel.

This stage is the heart of the OPD funnel.

It's not about how advanced your treatment is; it's about **emotional safety**. The consultation room becomes a psychological space where patients unconsciously ask:

"Will this doctor judge me? Rush me? Understand me? Or will they truly be on my side?"

Regrettably, the irony is, most doctors are never taught to manage this emotional terrain. They are taught merely to open the patient file, look at test reports, ask a few textbook questions, and start typing.

In this process, **something critical gets missed: the patient's story**. Their fears, their family pressure, the Google search spiral they've been stuck in.

If you don't give space for this story to emerge, the consultation becomes a transaction, not a relationship.

That's why the first two minutes are sacred. Let the patient speak uninterrupted. Make eye contact. Don't hide behind the screen. Sit forward slightly, nod gently, and let them empty their mental burden. This is not wasted time; this is trust-building in action.

From Non-Existent To Trustworthy

A dedicated and brilliant pediatrician in Kota was facing a problem that many doctors quietly struggle with.

Parents would bring their children for a consultation, despite everything being great, from treatment to the clinic, the staff, and the location, the practice wasn't thriving as it should. Despite his solid clinical expertise, his new patient rate was barely 20%.

He was frustrated because he knew he was delivering quality care, but something was missing.

When we sat together to look into it, I immediately **spotted two leaks in his funnel.**

1. His awareness stage was weak. The clinic had a plain board and a basic Google listing with only three reviews.

   Parents in his area didn't even know he existed.

- We started by optimizing his Google My Business profile with photos of his child-friendly waiting area.
- Added ten real reviews from happy parents to the profile.
- And created one simple awareness reel: "Three mistakes parents make when giving fever medicine to kids."

Within two weeks, the reel crossed 12,000 local views. Parents began to recognize his name before stepping into the clinic.

2. The second leak was in the consultation stage. I observed that his first five minutes with patients were very transactional.

   He would quickly go through reports and prescribe medicines. The parents, still anxious, left feeling unheard.

   We restructured his consultation flow.

   Instead of opening with reports, he began by asking a simple question:

   "What worries you the most about your child right now?"

That one line opened the floodgates. Parents spoke for two minutes without interruption, and he responded with reassurance before moving to clinical details.

One mother, whose child had recurrent coughs, later told him:

"Doctor sahab, this was the first time I felt someone understood my fears instead of just giving syrups."

She returned for every follow-up, brought her younger child for regular check-ups, and even referred three families from her housing society.

Within three months, his return rate had jumped to 87%.

What changed wasn't his prescription; it was how he guided parents through the ACCRF funnel. From awareness (a reel and reviews), to consideration (trust signals and testimonials), to consultation (listening before treating), every stage worked together.

He later told me,

"I thought I needed more patients. What I really needed was to stop losing the ones already coming."

One thing we've seen at **Rungta Hospital** is that when patients feel *heard,* half their symptoms feel lighter even before a prescription is given. That's why we train our staff and doctors not just in clinical skills but in **empathy-first interaction**. Whether it's a nurse saying, *"Don't worry, the doctor will explain everything in simple terms,"* or a specialist drawing on paper to show how a condition works, the goal is always the same: **make the patient feel safe, smart, and supported.**

Even small things like how chairs are placed, how much physical distance is kept, or whether the doctor sits on a higher or equal level send unconscious signals.

The next part of the consultation, explaining the diagnosis, is where even the best doctors are likely to lose the patient accidentally.

Watch out for these silent killers-

- Using difficult technical terms.
- Rushing through the explanation.
- Or worse, just saying, *"Take these and come back in 5 days,"* without offering reassurance.

But here's the truth: **understanding = power.**

When patients understand what's happening in their body in their own language, they trust the treatment more and comply better.

And finally, the goodbye moment. This is where the memory is sealed. **Instead of saying "Okay, we're done." Say something that gives hope and support. Try:**

"You've already taken the right first step; we'll handle the rest together."

Or

"You're not alone in this. We'll walk through every stage with you."

At Rungta, we often say internally:

"A patient's healing begins not with the medicine, but with the moment they feel they're in the right hands."

And that's what we aim to deliver in every consultation: a sense that they're not just a case number, but a human being with a story, a struggle, and a right to be heard with compassion.

Because ultimately, no matter how many tests you prescribe or how advanced your machines are, the consultation is a **human moment.** And when done right, it doesn't just bring healing, it brings loyalty.

3

CHAPTER

FROM SECOND VISIT TO SUPERFAN: THE SILENT ENGINE OF OPD GROWTH

Most doctors focus on getting more patients. They invest time, money, and effort into visibility, awareness, and marketing. But what they often miss is that the biggest threat to their OPD growth is not outside; **it's what happens after the first visit.**

- A patient walks in, listens attentively, thanks you sincerely, and walks out.
- There's no dissatisfaction.
- No complaint.
- No red flag.

But they never come back. This isn't rare.

A global McKinsey study found that more than 50 percent of patients never return to the same doctor after their first visit, not because the treatment was wrong, but because they didn't feel emotionally anchored.

It's not a clinical failure. It's a relational one.

What's even more eye-opening is this: a report by Bain & Company shows that in**creasing retention by just 5 percent can improve profitability by 25 to 95 percent in healthcare businesses** . That means keeping existing patients just a little longer is more valuable than bringing in dozens of new ones.

Doctors who pay attention to this start seeing a different pattern.

The patient who returns for a second visit is ten times more likely to return and three times more likely to refer someone.

That second visit is not just a check-in. It's a turning point.

It is proof of trust. It's the moment where the relationship starts to shift from professional to personal.

Stage 4- Retention

The Engine of Compounding Trust

Retention is where most OPD strategies either succeed or silently collapse.

This is the stage where your patient either forgets you exist or starts building a bond so strong that they stay for years and bring others with them.

Let's start with the reality: retention doesn't happen on its own. You have to engineer it.

The first lever is follow-up.

Clinics that follow up within 48 hours of the first consultation, not to remind, but to show care or affinity, see massive differences.

A simple message like, "We hope you're feeling better. Do let us know if anything seems off?" works better than a generic "come again" pitch. In several case studies across India, this kind of **warm check-in increased revisit rates by 25 to 40 percent in under 3 months.**

But follow-up only works if the first consultation ends with the doctor planting the next step.

Instead of saying, "Come if needed," say, "Let's track your recovery together." I'd like to see you in five days." That sentence changes the mental frame. It no longer feels optional. And if your reception team books a return visit on the spot, you've closed the loop.

In clinics that implement this seriously, revisit rates go from under 40 percent to over 70 percent. That's not marketing. That's the process.

The next lever is **recognition**. When a patient returns, greet them like you remember them. A small "Good to see you again" lands deeply. According to a 2023 Deloitte report, 81 percent of patients say they are more likely to return to a doctor if they feel personally valued. That's a reminder that retention is emotional before it is logistical .

Now comes the most ignored part: the third visit.

By the time a patient visits you three times, they are emotionally aligned. They trust your rhythm. They're no longer testing you.

That's your opportunity to activate the next gear: advocacy.

Here, subtle scripting works. **Ask for feedback after the third visit.** If they are happy, invite them to share. Not in a pushy way. Just a simple "Would you be okay sharing your experience for others who might be scared like you were?" You'd be surprised how many patients say yes.

These short videos or messages, if placed on your reception TV, WhatsApp stories, or Instagram reels, act as social proof. Across departments like physiotherapy and general surgery, hospitals report that 50 to 60 percent of new patients walk in because of stories they saw or heard, not ads, not hoardings, not influencer campaigns.

And when that patient refers someone, close the loop again. A thank-you message. A call. A text, "We saw your cousin today - thank you for trusting us."

The Indian Journal of Community Medicine in 2021 confirmed that in Tier 2 and Tier 3 cities, the number one factor for choosing a doctor remains trust-based personal referrals–more than price, location, or even digital visibility.

When I interact with doctors, they often ask me, "What's my best marketing investment?"

The answer is simple. Retention. Because the cost of acquiring one new patient is five to seven times more than keeping an existing one.

Your most powerful strategy is not how to get more people to look at you. It's how to get the right people to stay with you. Because when they do, they bring others. Not through paid ads. Through shared belief. And that's how you quietly build the most respected, most trusted, and most unstoppable OPD in your city.

Stage 5- Fan

When Your Patient Becomes Your Brand

Fan-making begins when the patient no longer sees you as just a service provider, but as someone who stands apart from the rest, someone they admire, trust, and want to talk about. And this shift doesn't happen by accident. It happens when you deliberately plant signals of expertise, care, and emotional depth at key points in the patient journey.

Here's one of the most powerful shifts: instead of saying "I'm giving you this treatment," say, "In the last 12 months, I've helped over 300 patients with this exact issue, and this protocol has worked with most of them." **That's called social proof + credibility bundling.** It reassures the patient that they're not your first experiment. They're walking a path that's been tested, proven, and refined.

You can even go one step further and say, "Interestingly, a Harvard study published last year showed that 70 percent of similar cases improve faster when XYZ is combined with lifestyle changes. That's why I'm recommending this to you, too." Now you're not just treating, they're getting **Harvard-backed care.** You've positioned yourself as someone who reads, updates, and brings global science into your local cabin.

Let me now unfold another strategy that could be the game-changer for you.

Leveraging The Power of Your Expertise Through A book

Imagine you're a gastroenterologist. You've written a small 40-page booklet titled **"The Real Gut Truth: 7 Myths Your Stomach Wants to Tell You."** This doesn't need to be a published book; it could be a high-quality printed guide with your name and photo. On a patient's third visit, you hand it to them and say, "Since you're serious about your health, I want you to have this. I've written it from my years of treating gut issues just like yours." That moment creates **authority + intimacy**. It signals that you're not just treating symptoms, but leading them on a mission. And when your book is visible in your cabin or waiting area, every patient waiting sees it and feels they are in the hands of someone who's *respected, thoughtful, and different.*

Now, let's talk about **personalized surprise touchpoints,** a simple but rarely used fan-building strategy. On the patient's birthday or festival, your assistant sends a message like, "Wishing you good health and happiness this Diwali from Dr. Ramesh and team." Imagine how a patient feels when their doctor remembers them at a festival. That's fan psychology 101: **make them feel valued beyond the clinic.**

Another underestimated but deeply effective method is **"slow-building affinity."** In the first two visits, you focus on solving their medical issue. But from the third onward, you sprinkle small personal references: "Last time you mentioned your son was preparing for exams, how did they go?" or "Were you able to start that evening walk we discussed?" These lines signal memory and emotional investment, which deepen the connection. A fan is built when they feel like they're part of a journey *with you*, not just visiting *you*

By the fourth or fifth visit, when the trust is visible, when they smile, talk openly, or ask for your opinion on unrelated health matters, you're in the zone to **activate the referral ask**. But don't say, "Can you send patients?" Say, "I'm trying to help more people like you avoid unnecessary procedures. If you know someone who's suffering silently, I'd be happy to guide them." This approach is **non-pushy, purposeful, and specific**. You're not asking for numbers; you're offering your expertise where it matters.

And when patients become fans, treat them like insiders. Tell them softly, **"We're working on launching a preventive gut health camp next month. You'll be the first to know."** That one line makes them feel part of your inner circle, not just a visitor. Even if they don't attend, they will talk about it.

Ultimately, patients become fans not because of what you do, but how you do it again and again.

Turning Parents into Promoters

Remember the brilliant paediatrician in Kota struggling with bringing in new patients in the previous chapter.

Correcting the leaks in the awareness and consultation opening stage, his new patient walk-ins grew quickly, but then he faced another frustrating roadblock. Parents often came with their children once but rarely returned, even for routine checks.

Well, apart from the first two leaks in his funnel, we suggested one other small change to him.

- Instead of ending the consultation with "Come back if there is any issue," he began saying,
- **"I would like to see your child again in ten days, just to make sure everything is on track."**
- Alongside this, he set up a WhatsApp follow-up where his assistant sent a warm check-in message 48 hours after the visit.
- Within three months, they noticed that 90% percent of parents were returning for the second visit.
- Soon after, new referrals went up really high with existing parents saying, **"This doctor actually remembers us and checks on our child."**

His OPD doubled not because of ads, but because his patients felt guided and cared for.

By combining-

- Scientific depth
- Emotional intelligence
- Personal memory
- And soft authority cues like books, content, and connection.

You stop being just another doctor. You become the one they compare everyone else to.

This is what makes them stay. This is what makes them refer. This is what turns your OPD into a movement of stories.

4

CHAPTER

REDESIGNING YOUR CLINIC EXPERIENCE WITHOUT SPENDING A FORTUNE

Doctors often assume that OPD growth is about advertising, but one of the most powerful growth tools is right in front of you, your clinic itself.

The design of your space, the messages it conveys, and the emotions it triggers all play a silent but decisive role in whether patients come back, trust you, and refer others.

But most doctors upgrade their clinic by changing furniture, painting walls, or adding equipment. But the truth is, your clinic's **design doesn't start with things; it starts with emotions**. At every step of the patient's journey, they're *feeling* something and silently asking questions. If you can predict these emotions and respond to them through the space, you win loyalty without needing a massive budget. And the best part? You don't need to spend a fortune. You just need to be intentional.

Before you think of redesigning your clinic, ask yourself one question:

What do I want my patients to feel, step by step, as they enter, wait, meet me, and leave?

This is your blueprint. This blueprint will automatically suggest to you ideas on what you have to do to achieve it. As you have set your subconscious mind to think in a direction. Because every patient walking into your clinic is silently experiencing a journey, one that can either build trust or deepen doubt. Your space either becomes your silent partner in healing or your silent killer in patient drop-offs.

Let's begin where every patient journey starts, your entrance.

The first few seconds matter more than most doctors realize.

At the entrance, your goal should be to spark confidence.

The first impression is not just visual; it's emotional.

Patients are subconsciously thinking,

- "Am I in the right place?
- Is this doctor qualified enough for my problem?"

You answer that not with marble floors and great interiors but with authority cues.

Obviously, the marble flooring is also needed, but if the foundational part of things is not strong, just focusing on the interiors won't help.

To strip the objections,

- **You could place a standee or clean poster** showing your years of experience, specialties, any awards, and how many patients you've treated. A simple visual like "12+ years, 7,200+ patients, 3 international recognitions" tells your story instantly.
- **You can add a QR code linking to a one-minute video** where you introduce yourself and your care philosophy, a low-cost but high-trust way to humanize your brand.
- **Another idea is to display photos of your participation in conferences, awards you've received, or community events you've supported.** These visuals silently say, "*You're in safe hands*". As in Rungta hospital, in the digital creatives, we also try to portray our achievements of having 12,000+ Google reviews with a 4.8 rating, and we have treated more than 10 lakh 81 thousand + patients till date, which increases the confidence in the patients.

Research Backs The Power of Subtle Communication

In a 2022 study by the *Indian Journal of Clinical Practice*, over 61% of patients reported that seeing professional milestones displayed at the entrance made them feel safer and more confident about the doctor.

Moving into the waiting area, your goal is to *strip the patient's mental objections without saying a word.*

Most patients have silent fears-

- "Will they overcharge me?",
- "Will I get the right treatment?",
- "Is this clinic professional or commercial?"

Instead of leaving them to guess, use your walls to answer.

- Create a **testimonial gallery:** not just any feedback, but ones that directly tackle common doubts.
- For example, a framed testimonial that says, **"I thought the treatment would be too expensive, but they explained everything clearly and didn't push unnecessary tests,"** speaks volumes to a nervous first-timer. Play short, edited **video testimonials** on a looped TV in the waiting area, real patients sharing recovery stories. These act as objection-stripping tools, building trust more effectively than any brochure.
- **You can also turn your waiting area into a space of transparency.** Near the billing desk, post a printed sheet titled *"5 Common Billing Frauds in Hospitals, and Why We Never Do Them."* Explain in simple language things like duplicate charges, unnecessary tests, and inflated

consumables, and clearly state that your clinic has written policies against all of them.

This one small sheet can build immense trust.

- Another idea is to display a sample patient bill, clearly broken down with charges and explanations. Transparency is rare in healthcare, so when you offer it upfront, patients begin to trust you before they've even met you

From Chaos to Calm & Safety

How a Surgeon Transformed His Waiting Room

A general surgeon in a tier-3 city believed his OPD was not growing because of competition.

However, when we interviewed patients, a different truth emerged:

- They were frustrated by his cramped, noisy waiting area.
- Some left before their turn because the environment was stressful.

Instead of a costly renovation, we suggested three changes.

- Investing in clean, comfortable seating,
- Adding soft instrumental music
- And placing a digital screen with rotating slides on common health tips.

The effect was immediate.

- Patients reported feeling calmer, more respected, and more confident about the practice.
- Within six months, his reputation in the city improved, and referrals increased.

Patients said,

"If a doctor takes this much care outside the consultation room, imagine how he treats inside."

Just before the consultation room, reinforce your authority again. This is a subtle but critical space, where anxiety peaks. The patient has waited, possibly Googled their symptoms, maybe overheard others in distress, and is about to meet the doctor for the first time.

Their minds are full of doubts:

- "Will this doctor understand me?"
- "Will he rush through?"
- "Will I be told something scary?"

This is where a **second standee**, authority poster, or digital screen can speak on your behalf before you even say a word. Highlight your specialization results in plain language: "3,200+ cases of chronic back pain treated with a 92% improvement rate." Or "Trusted by 9,000+ patients across 22 cities."

Don't just write degrees or designations. Use numbers and outcomes, because what people remember is scale and success.

Another subtle but powerful tool here is a **"Did You Know?" wall,** not medical jargon, but patient-friendly facts that reduce fear. For example: "Did you know? 85% of vertigo cases are inner-ear related, not brain-related, and can be resolved with simple treatment." "One in three acidity cases are actually caused by stress, not food. Let's fix the root, not just the symptoms." These nuggets shift perception. You're no longer just a doctor; you're a calm educator. And educating before treating creates a sense of safety.

Now, once inside the consultation room, the energy should shift from *authority* to *affinity*. The patient should now feel: *This doctor understands me. I can open up.* Begin by removing physical barriers. Keep your chair at the same level, maintain eye contact, and listen without interrupting for the first 30–60 seconds. That alone sets you apart. But let's go further.

Have a framed one-page letter from you on the wall, titled "Why I Became a Doctor" or "What I Want Every Patient to Know." It can be personal, emotional, and even a bit vulnerable. This builds instant trust. It shows the patient that behind the stethoscope is a human being who cares. It can say things like: "My mother's illness is what made me choose medicine. I still remember how confused she felt when doctors used big words. That's why I promise to always explain things clearly."

Next, keep a small, branded guide on your desk, something you've written yourself. It doesn't need to be long, even 4 pages. For a gastroenterologist, it could be "Understanding Gut Health in 5 Simple Steps." For an orthopedician, "Back Pain Myths,

What You Need to Know." For a diabetologist, "How to Eat Sugar Right." Give it away **on the second or third visit** as a gift. The emotional message: *I care for your understanding, not just your labs.* You now become the **expert they quote in front of others,** "Mere doctor ne yeh likha hai..."

If you want to go one level deeper, **create a patient journey chart,** a printed flowchart, or a wall-mounted graphic behind you.

For example:

- **"For acidity:**

  Step 1: Lifestyle correction.

  Step 2: Medication.

  Step 3: Long-term gut healing."

It gives the patient a map. They know you have a method — not a trial-and-error approach. This drastically increases their faith in your treatment, and studies show that patient satisfaction doubles when they understand the roadmap of their care..

Finally, your **desk and room itself can carry subtle cues of warmth and mastery.** Keep one or two **handwritten thank-you cards** from past patients on your table. Display one framed success story like a patient photo with a note: "After 8 years of chronic pain, finally got relief. Thank you!" These aren't decorations. They are **emotional anchors.** They tell the next patient: *You are not alone. People like you have healed here.*

The medicine counter is often the last stop in a patient's journey through your clinic, but it's also the first place where doubts about cost and transparency begin to arise. That's why it's critical to design this area with one emotion in mind: **clarity and**

closure. By the time a patient reaches the pharmacy, they've seen the doctor and are likely either relieved, uncertain, or still anxious.

At this stage, they're silently asking-

- "Am I being overcharged?"
- Or "Is this safe and reliable?"

Your design and communication here must preempt these doubts and reassure them, without waiting for them to ask.

Taking Doubt Out of The Equation Smartly

Start by installing a framed poster near the pharmacy titled something like "5 Common Medical Billing Frauds" and How We Avoid Them." This could include lines like: charging for medicines not prescribed (×), inflating MRP (×), or pushing unnecessary branded drugs (×). Beneath it, list what you do differently: "We bill exactly at MRP," "All medicines are doctor-approved," or "We offer branded and generic options — you choose." According to Edelman's 2022 India Trust Barometer, ***71% of patients say they feel hospitals are not transparent about billing****. This single poster can flip that perception and position you as one of the few who care about ethics more than margins.*

- On the counter itself, add a bold but neat sticker: "No Hidden Charges. MRP-Based Pricing Only."
- If you offer senior citizen discounts, put that visibly too.
- These visual cues aren't just for show; they directly speak to the unspoken fears of exploitation that patients carry.

- Alongside, ensure your staff has a small, consistent script. Even a simple three-line flow like: "These are your prescribed medicines… Here's how to take them… call us anytime if you have doubts," builds trust instantly. You're not just dispensing medicine — you're providing guided care.

Ultimately, the medicine counter is not just about medication; it's about messaging.

When done right, it can transform a passive patient into a returning one, simply because they felt respected, informed, and valued at the very last moment. Let your competitors compete on price or variety. You win on **trust, transparency, and thoughtful care,** and that's what builds a brand patients recommend

5

CHAPTER

THE ONLINE OPD: WHERE TRUST IS BUILT BEFORE ENTRY

In this chapter, I'm going to share the untapped power of social media not as a place to waste time, but as a tool to 3X your OPD. Most doctors think marketing means running an ad or posting a festival greeting, but real growth comes when social media becomes your second OPD. Here, patients see you, hear you, trust you, and book even before meeting you. You'll understand which platform to use, how to use it, and what content builds authority before the first handshake

Facebook

Let's begin with the platform where most doctors already are, but few use **Facebook to their advantage effectively**. With over 440 million active users in India, Facebook is still a giant, especially among the **35+** age group. This is the same population that fills up your clinic. But what do most doctors do? They post Diwali wishes once a year, maybe a health camp poster, and that's it.

Facebook is not a notice board. It is a bridge between your clinic and your community. Use it effectively.

Take the example of this brilliant Doctor I met in Kolkata.

Building a Local Following

A cardiologist in Kolkata was posting regularly, but nothing was happening. When we spoke, I asked him,

"Do your patients even know you're on Facebook?"

He realized they didn't.

We made one small change: at the end of every consultation, he began saying,

"Sir/Ma'am, we share useful tips and alerts on our Facebook page. I'd love for you to follow us; it will help you stay updated."

Within a month, his page grew by 200 genuine followers: patients, not strangers. He posted short tips like "5 signs your BP is out of control & impacting your heart" and "Monsoon precautions for Heart-Health."

His patients started sharing the posts with family. Not only did his OPD grow, but he also became the doctor whom people in his city recommended online.

YouTube

Now let's talk about the most underrated platform in the medical field, YouTube. Did you know that health is one of the top 3 most-searched topics on YouTube India? More than 500 million users go there for answers. They don't want medical jargon; they want clear, human explanations.

From Showcasing Skill to Offering Solutions

I once spoke to a surgeon who said, "I've uploaded 10 surgery videos, but no one watches." I watched one. It was a 45-minute silent video of an operation. I told him, "You're showing skill, not solving fear."

When I met him, I told him, "You're showing skill, not solving fear."

We changed strategy.

His next video was just three minutes long:

"When should you worry about appendix pain?" **It was conversational and clear.**

In two weeks, it had 8,000 views.

Soon, a family drove in from 100 km away, saying, "Doctor, we saw you on YouTube and trusted your explanation."

At Rungta Hospital, too, patients have come from Bihar, Gujarat, and even Madhya Pradesh after watching a simple, useful video.

YouTube magnifies your credibility far beyond your city if you focus on clarity, not complexity.

Instagram

Next is Instagram, where 250+ million Indians are scrolling every day. Fast, stylish, and full of opinions, Instagram is where people form impressions quickly. If your practice involves aesthetic services, dermatology, IVF, weight loss, or dental care, Instagram is your digital reception desk. Here, the goal is not to educate deeply, but to make people stop, look, and feel a spark of trust.

Instagram works, but only if your content is relevant, short, and emotionally triggering, as the real-world example of a dermatologist shared below shows.

The Dermatologist Who Switched to Reels

While talking to a dermatologist, she told me, **"Patients expect instant cosmetic results. If acne doesn't clear in 2 weeks, they jump to another dermatologist. Social media promises quick fixes, but in reality, treatment takes time. Because of this impatience, my growth is limited."**

So, I told her that if social media is misleading your patients, why don't you use social media to counter this, to educate your clients on the value of commitment and patience in skincare?

She said she was using Instagram regularly, but getting no results.

The reason was that she used to post long captions & posts explaining skincare. **Her engagement was low, and she thought Instagram was overrated.**

We asked her to make 2 shifts

1. Shifted her to short reels like

- "3 foods that trigger acne."
- "Myth vs Truth: Sunscreen indoors."
- "Dark circles: 3 real causes."

One reel crossed 90,000 views. Within three weeks, her clinic calls doubled.

2. We asked her to start her own Podcast where she could educate and mold her clients to better understand what to expect from their treatment.

This worked double fold, the viral reels kept the patients rolling in, and the valuable information and education she shared on her podcasts helped them stay committed to their treatment plans and not keep hopping clinics.

Instagram is not about lecturing. It is about sparking recognition and building instant recall.

LinkedIn

And then there's the platform most doctors ignore: LinkedIn. This isn't where patients come. But this is where hospital owners, investors, pharma leaders, and high-ranking professionals are watching.

The Intensivist Who Went Global

A critical care specialist once posted a detailed note on a rare ICU case he had managed.

- A month later, a healthcare group in Dubai reached out, saying they had been following his posts.
- That single connection led to speaking opportunities and an eventual consulting offer.
- He had never imagined LinkedIn could impact his career. But this is its quiet power:

It positions you as a thought leader and builds invisible credibility among influential circles.

That's LinkedIn's quiet power; it builds reputation, networks, and unseen respect.

So, what does each platform do for you?

- **Facebook:** Builds emotional trust with your local patient base.
- **YouTube:** Establishes you as an authority in your specialty.
- **Instagram:** Creates aspiration and visibility for niche practices.
- **LinkedIn:** Positions you as a thought leader and opens doors to bigger opportunities.

But here's the secret: You don't have to do everything.

Just do what fits your personality, your patients, and your goals. If your OPD thrives on elderly patients, Facebook and YouTube are gold. If you're into cosmetic care, Instagram is your clinic's face. If you're looking to scale, network, or partner, LinkedIn is your conference room.

And remember, your patients may not tell you they saw your post, but they did. Your content is your new reputation.

Now that you know where your patients are, it's time to learn what to say to them. Because posting for the sake of posting won't get you patients. You need a content strategy rooted in value, frequency, and trust-building. In the next chapter, I'll show you how to create content that doesn't just get likes but converts trust into footfall.

6

CHAPTER

TURNING YOUR SOCIAL MEDIA INTO A SILENT OPD BUILDER

In the last chapter, we explored where your patients are. We decoded which platform serves what purpose.

Now that you know where to show up, it's time to understand how to show up.

When I first joined the hospital, one of the most confusing and frustrating areas was digital marketing.

We were spending money on agencies, running ads, making posts, and yet, the OPD barely moved.

I couldn't understand what was going wrong. So I did what I always do when something doesn't add up: I went deep. I took personal mentorship from some of India's best digital marketing coaches. I didn't just learn how to run ads; I learned how patient psychology works online, how conversion actually happens, and what 95% of doctors are doing wrong without realizing it.

While building this book, I interviewed over 500+ doctors across India. And again and again, one pain point came up: "We're spending lakhs on digital marketing, but we have no idea if it's even working." Many said their agencies sent them reports every month, impressions, reach, likes, and even CTR. But none of that translated into actual OPD growth. That's when I realized something crucial: digital marketing has become a blind spot in healthcare

Most agencies optimize for the wrong goals. They make you feel good with metrics - likes, shares, comments, but those numbers don't build trust or drive footfall. Your OPD doesn't grow because these metrics don't reflect reality. Effective digital marketing for doctors should focus on engaging conversations, making calls, and driving conversions. Not pretty designs. Not festival wishes. Not reels with trending music. Most agencies treat your clinic like they treat a gym or a clothing brand. They post quotes, festival wishes, generic stock content, or "Good Morning" reels. And you're left wondering why no new patients walked in. But the problem is not that digital doesn't work; it's that nobody is showing you how it should be done differently for healthcare.

Now let's talk about what actually works.

Here's something no agency will tell you: the goal isn't visibility, it's emotional connection.

Patients scroll with fear in their minds and doubt in their hearts.

Your content has to dissolve those doubts.

For example, instead of saying "Expert in Gastroenterology," say, "Confused between gas and something serious? Here's how to know when to see a doctor."

Teach, don't just promote.

The moment you become a guide, not just a service provider, your content starts working. One ENT specialist I interviewed started a reel series called "Don't Panic," where she explained common but scary symptoms in 30 seconds. In just 3 weeks, she had three new walk-ins who said, "We saw your reel and felt you'd understand our problem."

Now, what's the first rule: always design your digital marketing with one goal,

"How can I move this patient from curiosity to trust to action?"

Everything else is noise. In my experience and learning, there are six campaign types that consistently work when done properly.

1. **First, Objection-Removal Reels.** These are short 30–60 second videos where you address a patient's most common fears. For example, *"Kya bypass surgery zaroori hai?"* (Is bypass surgery necessary?)or *"Back pain ka matlab slip disc nahi hota."* **(All back pain does not mean a slipped disc!)** These reels work because they reduce fear, offer clarity, and build trust. They should always end with a subtle invitation, like "Confused about your next step? Book a clarity consultation with us."
2. **Second, Local Case Study Ads.** You don't need celebrity videos. Just share real transformations from your clinic. For example, "Mrs. Jain came to us with knee pain that made walking difficult. After 3 sessions of physiotherapy, she climbed stairs without pain." These work better than any brand campaign. People don't want promises; they want proof.
3. **Third, WhatsApp Micro-Campaigns.** This is the most underrated strategy. Collect numbers from all OPD patients and referrals. Then, every 2–3 weeks, send a short useful message like "How to spot early signs of sugar-related nerve pain (Read in 1 minute)" with a link to your content. Or you could run custom ads on Facebook on these contact numbers; this would act as TOMR (Top of the mind recall). This isn't selling it's staying in their mind.
4. **Fourth, another mistake doctors make is blindly boosting posts without knowing where they're going.** If your clinic is in Jaipur, but your video is reaching

people in Delhi, Kolkata, and Hyderabad, it's money wasted. You need to run hyperlocal campaigns, targeting people within a 5–8 km radius. But even here, most agencies make another mistake: they don't follow up. Let's say someone clicks your ad or watches your video. What happens next? Nothing. That's the leak. The funnel breaks. What you should ask for is retargeting: if someone watches 50% of your reel, show them your clinic video next. If they click on your website, follow them with a second ad saying, "Still unsure? Book a free 5-minute consult." This warms them up. This builds familiarity. And this is exactly how consumer behavior works today — it's never a single-click decision.

5. **Fifth, Before-After Gallery or Journey Walls (also for digital).** On your Instagram, show the journey: day 1, week 1, week 4. Whether it's weight loss, post-op recovery, or ortho mobility, patients want to see the path. Do this for Instagram, but also build a printed version and place it in your waiting area, TV, or corridor standees. Repetition builds authority.

6. **Sixth, Doctor-as-Educator Campaigns.** You don't need to act like an influencer. But if you share even one data point or medical insight every week—like "Did you know 70% of chronic fatigue cases are misdiagnosed as anxiety?"—you slowly become the doctor who knows more. And trust follows knowledge.

Now, how do you guide your agency to run these?

Ask for a weekly performance review, not a PDF report. On the call, ask:

- How many OPD leads came directly or indirectly from last week's campaigns?
- Which content got the most engagement, and why?
- What are we posting next week, and what is the goal of each post?

Demand a content calendar that is strategy-led. You should be able to approve every week's topic in advance. Set themes: one patient story, one myth-busting reel, one WhatsApp tip, one doctor quote.

Also, tell your agency clearly: you don't need just 100K reach. You need 5 walk-ins. That's it. Let them reverse engineer how to make that happen. Most of the time, that means fewer posts, but better targeted, and with a better follow-up system.

A Bonus Hack

And here's one bonus hack: in your waiting area, install a small standee or wall frame that says, "Dr. [Name] answers the internet's top 5 questions on spine surgery. Scan to watch." Link it to a YouTube playlist. Now, your physical patients also become your digital followers, and followers become fans.

If your agency isn't thinking like this, they're not failing at digital. They're failing at understanding your business. You don't need to be everywhere. You just need to be clear, helpful, and visible to the right people, at the right time, with the right message.

7

CHAPTER

WHAT YOUR PATIENTS REALLY WANT: BUT NEVER SAY OUT LOUD

In the last few chapters, we talked about how patients go from strangers to superfans, how trust, follow-ups, small human gestures, and experience design help you build patient loyalty. But here's the hard truth: none of that works if you're guessing what your patient truly wants.

I've seen doctors assume they know their patients.

But assumptions are wrong 62 percent of the time.

What your patient tells you and what they actually feel are often two very different things.

I used to think I had a strong grip on patient psychology. But when I started personally interviewing patients purely to understand their mindset, I was shocked. Their expectations, worries, unspoken desires, and past frustrations painted a completely different picture than the one we build in our heads as providers.

That's why this chapter matters. Because if you want to 3X your OPD, you don't need better ads. You need better insight into what your marketing and patient journey systems should be built upon.

The "Patient Truth Formula": A New Lens

When I was interviewing so many patients, I created a simple but powerful 4-part formula to decode what your patient is really thinking.

It's the 4W formula, which includes:

1. **What They Expect:** The basics they assume should be there

2. **What They Wish:** The extra touches they secretly desire
3. **What They Fear:** The invisible barriers holding them back
4. **What They Remember:** Past wounds that still influence their trust

The 4W Formula For Understanding Your Patients Better

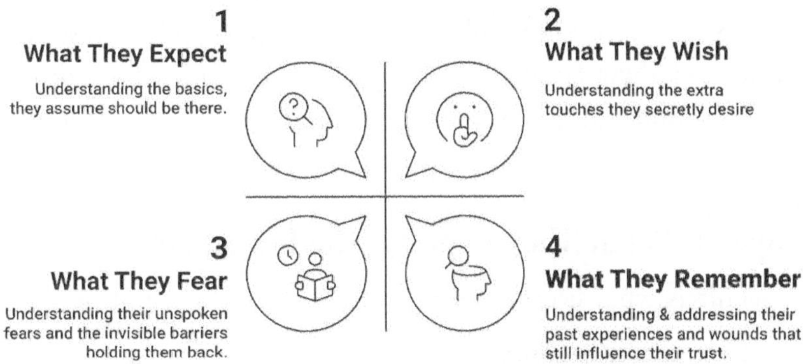

Each of these layers matters. And the deeper you understand their inner world, the faster your credibility and retention grow. But here's the most important part: you won't uncover any of this during a consultation. You need to set up an intentional patient interview.

Setting the Stage: How to Interview Your Patients the Right Way

Before anything, call or message the patient at least a day in advance. Ask for 45 minutes of their time.

You could say:

"I'm trying to improve how we serve people like you. I thought you were among the best patients to give me genuine feedback. I'd love to understand what worked, what didn't, and what you honestly feel when you visit a hospital. Can we meet for 45 minutes just to talk?"

Do this outside your OPD hours or on a light day. Bring a notebook. Keep your phone away and order some tea or coffee for them. And most importantly, don't jump into the interview directly.

Tip 1: Start informally. Ask about their background, their work, and their family. This helps both of you come onto the same ground emotionally. Once rapport is built, start peeling each layer.

Layer 1: What They Expect, The Essentials

This is what every patient already assumes should be there.

This could include:

- The doctor will listen patiently
- The diagnosis will be explained clearly

But don't guess, because there are many more things patients also expect.

Ask:

"When you visit a doctor, what are the things you feel must be there, no matter what?"

Tip 2: When they answer, don't stop there. Dig deeper.

If they say, "The waiting time should be less," follow up with: "Can you tell me what you consider timely treatment to be, 10 minutes, 20 minutes, or what?"

This reveals the intensity of their expectations and their emotional triggers. You should spend at least 10 minutes on this part.

Layer 2: What They Wish, The Extras That Build Loyalty

This is where you uncover things they don't ask for but would deeply value if offered. These are the small gestures that set you apart. In my interviews, I've seen mind-blowing ideas come up.

Before diving into questions, I explain what I mean with a relatable example: nowadays, having a phone is a need, but an iPhone is a wish. If you don't get the iPhone, your life won't stop, but if you do, it adds joy and satisfaction.

Similarly, I ask:

"What things do you think '*Yeh bhi mil jata toh accha rehta*'? (It would be great to have these), like maybe a recliner chair or someone to guide you during the process?"

Tip 3: Give prompts to help them think deeply.

Say:

"Like, suppose someone followed up with a WhatsApp message... would that help?"

Or:

"If someone sat with you during the tests to guide you, would that make you feel more comfortable?"

These desires are hidden loyalty triggers. But it is not possible to fulfill all the desires, but if you fulfill just one or two, you'll be remembered for years.

Layer 3: What They Fear, The Invisible Barriers

This is the part most doctors miss. Patients often don't talk about their fears unless asked directly and gently. But these fears silently affect whether they return, recommend, or even trust your treatment.

Start with a question like:

"Before coming to any doctor or hospital, what's something you're worried about, even if you don't say it out loud?"

Common answers I heard in interviews included:

- "They might overcharge me."
- "I might get admitted unnecessarily."
- "They'll push me for surgery."
- "I won't be able to afford the medicines."

These fears are often rooted in past experiences or stories from others. Once they open up, don't defend yourself, just listen.

Then dig deeper:

"Did something happen earlier that made you feel this way?"

Tip 4: Document these fears. They are your conversion killers. Use them to rework your communication, both verbal and non-verbal.

For example, if patients fear being overcharged, consider putting a framed poster near the billing desk that says: "Transparent Pricing. No unnecessary tests. Ask us anything."

Fears don't go away by explaining. They go away by proactively addressing them before the patient even brings them up.

Layer 4: What They Remember, The Past That Shapes the Present

Every patient walks in with emotional baggage. Some had bad experiences. Some felt neglected. Some carry trauma from how their family members were treated. These memories shape how they see you, even if you're not at fault.

Ask gently:

- "Have you ever had a bad experience with a doctor or hospital before?"
- "What happened, and how did it make you feel?"
- " Have you ever changed a hospital? If yes, why?"
- "If that hadn't happened, what would you have expected instead?"

These conversations may go deep, so take your time. Don't try to correct them, just understand. Because when you know the wound, you can design your experience to be its healing.

Tip 5: After collecting this data from a few patients, map the patterns.

You'll start seeing that many people have the same scars, and that gives you the clarity to make your OPD environment a place of reassurance, not just treatment.

The Gynecologist Who Discovered & Treated "Unspoken Need For Privacy"

A gynecologist in a mid-sized Rajasthan town could not understand why many first-time patients never returned.

We suggested using the 4W Framework through short, structured interviews.

- In one session, a patient revealed, "I didn't feel comfortable asking my questions as the door was open and I felt I would be heard outside by everyone in the reception area."
- Others admitted they wanted more privacy; one narrated an incident of how embarrassed she was when she was on the examination table waiting for the doctor, but someone walked in without even a knock.
- Some others said they needed a gentler and simpler explanation of their body functions and diagnosis so that they could understand easily.

These insights had nothing to do with the doctor's clinical skill.

Acting on this-

- First and foremost, the doctor ensured that the door was firmly closed once the patient was escorted in and comfortably seated.
- Next, the doctor gave explicit instructions to the staff that under no circumstances was anybody to enter the room during the consultation.
- If the doctor needed assistance, she began taking permission from the patient and duly introduced the nursing staff member to the patient, telling them that this was a safe space and they should feel free to ask their questions, as their privacy was valued.
- She began using simpler language in her interaction with her patients, and began ending every session with, "What concerns you the most about this treatment?"

Within four months, the revisit rate increased by 40 percent.

Patients started telling others,

"This doctor actually understands what we are afraid to say."

Insight First, Everything Else Later

You don't need to fix your marketing first. You need to fix your understanding. When you know what your patients truly expect, wish for, fear, and remember, you no longer need to guess what will work. You'll know.

And the best part? These interviews don't just help your OPD. They transform you as a doctor. They make you more human, more aware, and more trusted. That's where the real growth begins.

What Will You Choose to Do Next?

If you've reached this page, it means you've already done what most doctors don't: **you've invested time in understanding your patient's journey, not just your own profession**.

And now, you're standing at a fork in the road.

You can either close this book and start implementing the ideas one by one in your own clinic, because everything you need to 3X your OPD is already here. The frameworks, the scripts, the design tips, the retention techniques, and most importantly, the mindset shift.

Or –

You could take a shortcut. Not in effort, but in time. Because the truth is, what you've read here is only 20% of what I've learned after over 120 hours of interviews with patients, top-performing doctors, and some of the best marketing minds in India.

The rest can't all fit into a book. It lives in conversations, case-specific ideas, and small tweaks based on your specialty, city, and style.

So, here's my invitation:

If you've read this book and it sparked even a single new idea…

If you've made notes and genuinely want to grow your OPD with integrity… **Then I'd love to give you a free 10-minute strategy session, just one-on-one, just you and me. We'll sit down, talk about your practice, and I'll think with you.** Not just share more insights, but the right ones for you.

Or if you're ever in Jaipur, come visit us at Rungta Hospital. Just spend half a day walking through how we've applied many of these principles in real life, no filters, no slides, just real systems and real stories. Because I know you didn't come this far just to stay stuck. You want to become that doctor, the one patients never forget.

Let's make that happen.

Nityanand Rungta

Rungta Hospital, Jaipur

6350097784 nityanand@rungtahospital.com